THE MERRY WIVES OF WINDSOR

AN OPERA IN THREE ACTS

Text by

HERMANN von MOSENTHAL

(After Shakespeare's play)

Music by

OTTO NICOLAI

English Version
by
JOSEF BLATT

VOCAL SCORE

Ed. 2266

G. SCHIRMER

New York

NOTE

G. SCHIRMER, INC.
609 Fifth Avenue
New York, N.Y. 10017

44163

PREFACE

OTTO NICOLAI was born in Koenigsberg, East Prussia on June 9, 1810. He was not unknown when the first performance of *The Merry Wives of Windsor* took place, on March 9, 1849. For seven years he had been principal conductor of the Imperial Opera in Vienna—he founded the world famous Philharmonic concerts by the orchestra of that institution—and his two operas *Il Templario* and *Il Proscritto* were frequently performed. They were written in the grand Italian style to which the composer had been exposed during a long sojourn in that country when he was a young man. His contract with the Vienna Imperial Opera stipulated that he had to compose a German opera and he eagerly seized the opportunity. He searched for a suitable libretto and finally chose the Shakespearian comedy as a subject for a comic opera and began work in 1845. It was, however, a protracted labor in spite of the enthusiasm he brought to its composition. His busy schedule as one of the most renowned operatic and symphonic conductors of his day left him only little time to compose; and illness often interfered with his work. When he had nearly finished the opera the intendant of the Imperial Opera declined to perform it with the excuse that it was one year beyond the time stipulated in his contract. Offended, Nicolai resigned his position in Vienna and accepted an offer of the King of Prussia to direct the Dome Choir in Berlin and conduct at the Royal Opera House. There he led the first performance of his new opera. It did not find the critical acclaim which his other stage works had won. Three more performances of it in March were conducted by the composer. Its success with the audience was growing steadily. Nicolai died suddenly of a cerebral hemorrage, on May 11, 1849. He could not have imagined the tremendous acclaim with which the musical world was soon to receive his last work.

Only a year later the opera started its triumphal journey over all the German stages. Soon afterwards it found its way to the opera stages of other European countries, and remains one of the most beloved of all comic operas.

The reasons for this success are quite evident if one listens to a good performance of the opera. There are the many fresh and sweet Italianate melodies, the perfect balance of the artfully wrought concerted numbers, the sharp and humorous musical characterizations of persons and situations, and an amazingly colorful and sensitive orchestration. Then, too, there is the tight and fast moving libretto which uses only the main sections of Shakespeare's comedy. These virtues make it possible for *The Merry Wives of Windsor* to survive all manner of tampering with its original form, and to withstand the rivalry of such a masterpiece on the same subject as Verdi's *Falstaff*.

In the present translation I have endeavored to preserve the simple, straightforward style of the German lyrics and to leave unchanged the rhythm, accents and phrasing of the original vocal line. The dialogues, however, have been radically shortened in conformance with contemporary tastes, and to keep the audience's attention concentrated on the musical numbers of the opera.

The musical cuts incorporated in this edition are the ones generally made in performances everywhere. They occur in concerted numbers and are intended to tighten the dramatic progress. Except for these few cuts, however, the work does not need any doctoring, transposition or change of scenes. Experience has shown that, as with all master works, the best effect is achieved by performing it as was conceived.

In a letter to his librettist, H. S. Mosenthal, whose work the composer constantly supervised, Nicolai described the characters of his opera as follows: Mrs. Ford: a young, pretty, merry woman, 20 years old . . . Mrs. Page: a well preserved woman of 35, lively but less so than her friend, Mrs. Ford . . . Anne Page, her daughter, 17, much in love, beautiful, sentimental, but not too much so . . . Mr. Ford, 40, violent, very jealous and energetic. (The most important male part in the opera) . . . Fenton, 25, heart and head in the right place, really loves Anne . . . Mr. Page, 50, fat, very miserly, phlegmatic. Falstaff . . . Falstaff.

I am very grateful that this translation of this opera, originally made for performances by my opera classes at the University of Michigan, seems to have initiated a great number of performances by various organizations in this country. I hope that this wonderful work may soon find its rightful, permanent place in the repertory of the ever increasing number of American opera companies.

Ann Arbor, Michigan, September 1956

JOSEF BLATT

CAST OF CHARACTERS

SIR JOHN FALSTAFF . . . . *BASS*

MR. FORD . . . . *BARITONE*

MR. PAGE . . . . *BASS*

FENTON . . . . *TENOR*

SLENDER . . . . *TENOR*

DR. CAJUS . . . . *BASS*

MRS. FORD (ALICE) . . . . *SOPRANO*

MRS. PAGE (MEG) . . . . *MEZZO-SOPRANO*

ANN PAGE . . . . *SOPRANO*

A NEIGHBOR . . . . *TENOR*

Men, women and children.

Elves, spooks, insects.

The town of Windsor.

SYNOPSIS OF SCENES

ACT. I.   Scene 1. A court.
Scene 2. A room in Mr. Ford's house.

ACT. II.   Scene 1. A room in the Garter Inn.
Scene 2. The garden of Mr. Page's house.
Scene 3. Mrs. Ford's room.

ACT. III. Scene 1. A room in Mr. Page's house.
Scene 2. Windsor Forest.

THE MERRY WIVES OF WINDSOR

ACT I

Scene One: A court. Mrs. Ford informs her friend, Mrs. Page, that she has received a crude love letter from the unattractive and corpulent, Sir John Falstaff. Outraged, the women decide to teach him a lesson. They leave. Mr. Page and Mr. Ford enter, accompanied by two suitors of Mr. Page's daughter, Anne—timid Slender and blustering Dr. Cajus. Anne's true love, Fenton, appears and asks Mr. Page for her hand. The penniless suitor is rudely rejected, but defiantly vows he will wed Anne despite every obstacle.

Scene Two: Mr. Ford's house. Mrs. Ford awaits Falstaff. She and Mrs. Page have sent an anonymous note to her husband informing him of her rendezvous with Sir John. A large basket is brought in. Later, the frightened Falstaff is stuffed into it and dumped into the Thames River. The women's plan works out perfectly; the jealous Mr. Ford is embarrassed in front of his neighbors.

ACT II

Scene One: A tavern. Ford, disguised as a "Mr. Brook" visits Falstaff at the Garter Inn. He seeks Sir John's help to gain the favor of Mrs. Ford and offers him a purse for his assistance. Ford discovers that Falstaff had been at his home the preceding day, and that his wife has invited him to visit her again this very afternoon.

Scene Two: A garden. Anne's two unwanted suitors, Slender and Cajus, unknown to each other, plan to meet her during her daily walk in the garden. When Fenton arrives, they are forced to hide. The lovers, unsuspectingly watched, reaffirm their affection.

Scene Three: Mrs. Ford's room. Falstaff has just arrived when Mrs. Page announces the unexpected approach of Mr. Ford. Quickly, the resourceful women disguise Falstaff as an old woman, a relative of Mrs. Ford's maid. Mr. Ford has forbidden her presence in his house and in his anger, beats her mercilessly. He confidently searches for Sir John, but is again unsuccessful and ridiculed.

ACT III

Scene One: Mr. Page's house. The wives have informed their husbands of Falstaff's letter and his subsequent punishments. Ford has been forgiven his unwarranted jealousy. They decide to play another trick on Sir John. There is to be a masquerade and the wives are to meet him disguised as the legendary hunter, Herne, in Windsor Forest. Mrs. Page, alone with Anne, gives her a red elf's costume to wear. Cajus will then recognize her and they can elope. After Mrs. Page departs, Mr. Page enters with a green elf's costume. He has a similar plan; but it is Slender with whom Anne is to run off. Anne decides to give the costumes to Slender and Cajus, and steal away with Fenton.

Scene Two: Windsor Forest. The townspeople, disguised as spooks and spirits of the forest, await Sir John. He appears as Herne, with large antlers on his head. Mrs. Page and Mrs. Ford join him. When the ghosts approach noisily, the women run away leaving the terrified Falstaff to face his tormentors alone. He tries in vain to hide, and is pinched, stabbed and mocked. Sir John repents, the masqueraders are revealed and the opera ends on a note of laughter and merriment.

THE MERRY WIVES OF WINDSOR

Text by Hermann von Mosenthal
(after Shakespeare's play)
English version by
JOSEPH BLATT

Overture

Otto Nicolai

44163CX

Allegro vivace

12

15

44163

ACT I

A court. At the right, the house of Mr. Page; at the left, the house of Mr. Ford. In the background, a fence with a door through which the other side of the street may be seen. It is an afternoon in summer.

Scene 1

(Mrs. Ford appears from her house with an opened letter in her hand.)

No. 1 Duet

ug - ly and un-couth! May our good Lord protect ___ us.

in tempo

quasi parlando

I can't believe what

(she reads)

I am reading:

"Your beau-ty, dear, is fash-ioned Af-

ter my heart's de - sire. Your eyes look so im - pas-sioned And you seem full of

fire."

poco a piacere

in tempo

An im-pu-dent re-mark is this. My eyes are no con-cern of his

(continues reading)

"We both love liq - uor eve-ry day. That's per - fect, don't you

scamp, I see it clear-ly, And for these in-sults you'll pay dearly.

I shall consult with Mistress Page A-bout the plot that we shall stage. I shall consult with Mistress

Page A-bout the plot that we shall stage.

Scene 2

(Mrs. Page appears from her house also with an opened letter.)

MRS. PAGE

I have to find dear Mistress Ford, And she must see this let-ter.

24

44163

26

44163

end - - ed. Don't e-ven think of it, that would not help a bit. Don't e-ven think of

it, that would not help a bit. Well, you know best. Here is what I sug - gest.

MRS. PAGE   MRS. FORD

With woman's wit and craft-y thought _____ We'll set a trap to seize him.

And then when he is firm-ly caught _____ We shall de-ride and tease him.

MRS. PAGE

Oh yes, that's good.

With art _____ we'll set a trap to seize him.

With woman's wit and art We'll set a trap to seize. him,   And then when he is

We shall de-ride and tease him. So

caught, and then when he is firm-ly caught We shall de-ride and tease him. So

let us find a clev-er plan and then proceed as fast we can. Yes,

let us find a clev-er plan and then proceed as fast we can. Yes,

let us find a clev-er plan and then proceed as fast we can.

let us find a clev-er plan and then proceed as fast we can.

Allegretto vivo

Ras-cal, here is your un-do-ing. Our re-venge we shall at-tain.

Ras-cal, here is your un-do-ing. Our re-venge we shall at-tain.

Allegretto vivo

30

ras - cal, here is your un - do - ing. Our re - venge we shall at - tain.

ras - cal, here is your un - do - ing. Our re - venge we shall at - tain.

Yes, my lov - er, you'll dis - cov - er you made a mis - take.

Yes, my lov - er, you'll dis - cov - er you made a mis - take.

Yes, what a big mis - take you vi-

My lov - er, you'll dis - cov - er what a big mis - take you vi-

Poco più mosso

made. Ras - cal, here is your un-

made. **Poco più mosso**

44163

yes, what a big mis-take you made, the

my lov-er, you'll dis-cov-er_ what a big mis-take you made, the

big mis- -take that you have made. Wit and fancy, merry

big mis- -take that you have made. Wit and fancy, merry

jesting shall attract you to our bait. But, my lov-er, you'll dis-cov.-er the mistake that you have

jesting shall attract you to our bait. But, my lov-er, you'll dis-cov-er the mistake that you have

(Both go quickly into Mrs. Ford's house.)

made, *but too late.*

made, *but too late.*

Scene 3

(Enter Mr. Page and Slender)

Page: My dear Mister Slender, set your mind at rest. As far as I am concerned, my daughter will marry you and no one else.

Slender: *(sings)* O Anne, my darling.

Page: Of course, you know that my wife prefers that foolish Frenchman, Dr. Cajus. *(Mr. Ford and Cajus enter)*
Here he comes with Mister Ford.

Mr. Ford: Mister Page, I just saw our wives together. I wonder what mischief they are up to.

Mr. Page: Neighbor, why are you always so suspicious?

Mr. Ford: Oh, I don't mistrust my wife. But a man can be *too* confident. I keep my eyes open and when I once catch my wife — I better see what she is doing. Good day, sirs. *(He leaves)*

Fenton: *(Fenton enters)* Pardon me, Mister Page. May I have a word with you?

Page: Certainly, Mister Fenton.

Scene 4

No. 2 Recitative and Duet

DR. CAJUS (*furiously*)

Recitative

Son-in-law! Son-in-law! *Mort de ma vie.* That still is pre-ma-ture.

Certain-ement I kill *ce* Monsieur Slen-der and I surely win her for my-self *tout*

Allegro

(*runs off.*)

suite. — *Je jure* I shall *par tous les diab* - les.

MR. PAGE (*looks after him*)

Ho-ho! See that Frenc

Allegro

roost-er there. And you, what is it that you want, Sir Fen - ton?

pair. Sir, my love is true and ten - der.

E - ven so. But let me say— E - ven

Yes, my love is true and - ten - der.

(aside)

.so. But let me say— I must

MR. PAGE   FENTON

say, dear Mis - ter Slen - der is a bet - ter match for her. Please

Andante

hear me. If e - ven once ___ you've known the feel - ing of ar - dent

Ped.   Ped.   Ped.   Ped.

love, its joy and pain, Then to your heart ___ I'm now ap-peal-ing. Oh, do not

Ped.   Ped.

cresc. ed affrett. *rall.*

let _____ me ask in vain. Oh, do not let me, do not let me ask in

vain. Please don't de - ny _____ my pur - est crav - ings ___ and you will

not _____ de-plore this hour. _____ Though I'm not rich _____ in gold and

sav - ings yet I have youth ____ and faith and pow'r. ____ Yes, I have youth and faith and

MR. PAGE (*aside*)

pow'r. Now just lis - ten to his rav-ings. Slen-der has a lot of

38

savings. All my neighbors would a - gree there's no bet - ter man than

FENTON

Please, don't de - ny my pur - est

he. He has money laid a - side.

And he sure - ly can pro - vide.

crav - ings and you will not de - plore this

Yes, he makes, by all ac - counts, year - ly almost six hun - dred

hour. Though I'm not rich in gold and

pounds. Yes, he makes, by all accounts, yearly six hundred pounds.

savings, _____ yet I have youth _____ and faith and

If my Anne would take that man, she'd be — ver — y wealth - y

cresc.

pow'r. _____ Yes, I have youth and faith ____ and

then, yearly, __ six hundred pounds! If my Anne would take that man, she'd be ver - y wealthy then, quite wealthy

Andante con moto

pow'r. *poco rall.* You won't re-fuse? Oh please, be

then, year - ly six hundred pounds! **Andante con moto**

poco rall.

p

kind. *f* There is no man more true and tender.

I'm sor - ry, sir, there's one I have in mind. In -

f *p* *p* *f*

Allegro

tell you, neighbor, just watch out. I'll win her yet, I have no doubt.

day.

Allegro

I tell you, neighbor, just watch out. I'll win her yet, I have no doubt. I

tell you, neighbor, just watch out. I'll win __ her yet, I have __ no doubt. I'll

win __ her yet, I have _____ no doubt. Ho- ho. Though hardships still may

MR. PAGE

FENTON

MR. PAGE FENTON

lie be - fore us. So? Our love at last will be vic - to - rious. Well. And

MR.

PAGE FENTON

44163

44

44163

Change of Scene

A room in Mr. Ford's house. In the background are two doors; one leads into the hall and can be locked. There are two side doors. On the left, a screen; on the right, a large laundry basket. There is a closet with several skirts, etc. In the foreground, a table with candles on it and a chair nearby.

Scene 5

(Mrs. Ford enters from the side door.)

No. 3 Recitative and Aria

Come to my aid, wit, merry jesting, all play-ful no-tions. whims and for-titude.

Nothing's too strong if we can use it, so wicked men be punished without mer - cy. They are so dev'lish, a race so bad that we can never hurt them quite e-

nough. Es - pe-cial-ly that fat old sin-ner who tries to steal our hearts. Ha ha ha ha.

He shall re-pent it. But when he comes, what manner shall I use to greet him?

What kind of language? Ah! That's how I'll speak:

Larghetto

Se - duc — — — er, why are

you — in-tent to lead — a virtuous wife — a-stray? Say why, oh why? Se-

duc - - - er, your plead - - - ings should have been ig-

nored. Oh yes!— My scorn _____ should be your just re-

ward, should be— your just re-ward. A - las,

a woman's heart is weak, so weak. Your woo - ing is ____ so

sweet and kind. You sigh. . . . My heart's a-

tor act - ing's something I can do. A

dar - ing plan it is, that's true. And yet, for once, a

prank like this can't grieve me; For once,

a prank like this can't grieve me.

And yet, for once, a prank like this can't grieve me.

54

Scene 6

Mrs. Page: (*enters*) Is everything ready?

Mrs. Ford: Right away. (*calls*) John, Robert, bring the basket.

Mrs. Page: Pretty soon your husband will get my anonymous letter and then we can expect a spectacle here.
(*servants bring in the basket*)

Mrs. Ford: Now listen. When I call you come at once and take this basket.

Mrs. Page: It will be heavy.

Mrs. Ford: You carry it to the pond and there, quickly, empty the whole basket into the water. You understand? (*servants nod*)
Now go and wait for my call. (*servants exit*)

Mrs. Page: Splendid. And I shall hide behind this door.

Mrs. Ford: Quickly, here he is. And don't forget, speak loud. (*Mrs. Page leaves*)
Now come, my lover, you shall get your reward.

Scene 7

(*Falstaff enters and immediately bolts the door.*)

No. 4 Finale

Andante maestoso

44163

Poco più mosso

MRS. FORD (*pretends bashfulness*)

Oh, let me go, sir. I'm up-set.

How now, my heart, you trem-ble yet? Come, end _____ all doubt and sor - row and don't be shy with me.

MRS. FORD

You're sweet to-day. To-mor - row you won't remem - ber me.

FALSTAFF

As tru-ly as I'm not a

MRS. FORD

I don't be-lieve you, sir.

pos - er.

Sweet la - dy, come a lit - tle

(Mrs. Page appears at the door and listens.)

I don't be-lieve you, sir. I don't be-lieve you, sir. Meg Page, don't you love

clos-er.

FALSTAFF

her? Her? What? Child how you are talk - ing. Brr! ___ Are you in your right

(imitates a funny walk)

mind? You know the way she walks. ___ How I de-test that

Tempo I MRS. FORD

Well then, I am con-

kind. No no no no, *that* God for-bid. I would be cra-zy you'll ad-mit.

(Mrs. Page withdraws)

FALSTAFF

tent - - ed, my lov - - er, sweet and smart. ___ It's time that you re-

60

44163

Scene 9
(*Two servants enter with a pole to carry the basket.*)

Tempo

Hur-ry up, you two, and do as I in-struct-ed you.

(softly, to the servants)

You dump it in the pond near-by. Re-mem-ber?

MRS. PAGE

Just dump it in the pond near-by.

Ha ha ha ha. Now, ten-der lov-er, have your fun.

Ha ha ha ha. Now

Now, ten-der lov-er, have your fun. Now, ten-der lov-er,

ten - der lov-er, have your fun. Now, ten-der lov-er, now ten-der

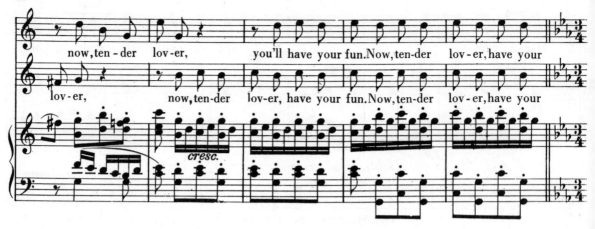

now, ten-der lov-er, you'll have your fun. Now, ten-der lov-er, have your

lov-er, now, ten-der lov-er, have your fun. Now, ten-der lov-er, have your

Scene 10

(As the servants are about to carry the basket out, Mr. Ford enters with Mr. Page, Cajus, Slender and several other men and women.)

Presto

fun.

fun.

MR. FORD *(furiously)*

Come in, you men, you wom - en, too. You

all shall wit - ness what I'll do. Come in, all you men, women, too. You all shall witness

what I'll do.

Hey, serv-ants, stop.

What do you want?

Be off.

Go to the bleaching pond.

MRS. FORD

(The servants carry the basket out.) MR. FORD MRS. FORD

How dare you? De - ceiv - er! How dare you? You're mad with

jeal - ous - y.

Kind - ly leave,you, my wash to me.

MR. FORD *(takes her by the hand)*

Ser - - pent, now at last you're caught.

Ser - - pent, now at last you're caught.

(to himself, but aloud)

Anne, my dar-ling. MR. FORD

And crown with might-y horns our brows.

MRS. FORD
Don't dis-grace your house. Dear-est spouse,

MRS. PAGE
Don't dis-grace your house. Be calm.

SLENDER
O Anne, my dar-ling.

MR. FORD
Yes, all women soon for-get their vows, I de-clare. All women

DR. CAJUS
Fu - - rieu - - se-ment. Il est ja-loux

MR. PAGE
Don't in-sult your spouse. Be calm.

Oh, what a fool-ish spouse. Ha ha

Oh, what a fool-ish spouse. Ha ha

Oh, what a fool-ish spouse. Ha ha

Ped. *

dear - est spouse, don't dis - grace your house.

Oh don't dis - - grace your house.

soon for - get _ their_vows and_crown_with_horns our brows.

fu - rieu - se - ment, *Il est ja - loux fu - rieu - se - ment.*

Oh don't in - - sult your spouse.

ha ha. What a jeal - ous, fool - ish spouse.

ha ha. What a jeal - ous, fool - ish spouse.

ha ha. What a jeal - ous, fool - ish spouse.

(Everybody exits, using both sides of the stage, except Mrs. Ford and Mrs. Page.)

MRS. PAGE

spite him. Oh yes. So let's pre-tend we're still in love _____ and for to-mor - row let's in - vite him. Oh, this is fun.

That's right. We shall pretend we're still in love.

We shall pre - tend we're still in love, to-mor-row, to-mor - row ___ we'll ___ a - gain ___ in - vite _____ him.

To - mor - - - row we'll a - gain ___ in-vite ___ him, to-mor - row ___ we'll ___ a - gain ___ in - vite _____ him.

poco rall.

col canto

you, We can be gay and yet be true, _ we can be gay and yet _ be

you, Yes, _ we can be gay and yet _ be

col canto

Scene 12

(Ford, and all the others, return.)

Più lento *(aside)* *rall.*

true. The hunters are re-turning and did not find their game.

true.

p *in tempo* *col canto*

(Mrs. Ford, weeping, MR. FORD *(to some men)*
MRS. PAGE *(secretly to her)* *rall.* sits down.)

Now all his pleading, spurning. Just weep in utter shame. Well?

col canto *in tempo* *mf* *p*

CHORUS MR. FORD *(to others)* CHORUS MRS. PAGE *(assisting Mrs. Ford)* MRS. FORD
(Tenors) (Basses) *(weeping)*

No. You? No. So tell me but a word, dear. I

mf *p*

44163

Più mosso

MRS. PAGE (*to Ford, accusingly*)

can - not bear this life. See here, how you have hurt her, your

poco meno

Allegretto

charming faith- ful wife. How could you be so rude? You

MRS. FORD (*rises*)

rall.

brute. You brute. You brute. Oh, oh, oh. Oh,

SLENDER

You brute. You brute.

DR. CAJUS,

You brute. You brute.

MR. PAGE

You brute. You brute.

Soprano

You brute.

Tenor

You brute.

Bass

You brute.

rall.

Andante

days _____ so sweet and gold - - en when I be-came his wife. I

nev - - er heard him scold - - ing and kind - - ness filled _____ our

life. Now eve - - ry wild sus - pi - cion can make _____ him storm _____ and

rall. **Tempo I** *stentate*

rave. His jeal - - ous dis-po-si - - - tion will send me to my

rall.

grave. It sends me to _ my grave, it sends _____ me to my

80

44163

Moderato

MR. FORD (*humbly*)

For - give, my sweet poor dar – ling, for - give. This let - ter made me

a piacere

Allegro

MRS. FORD (*suddenly getting up*)

fear that am - o - rous Sir John was here. He? What? I

col canto

shud — — — — — — der. I nev - er heard such

in - fa – my. Too — long have — I been pa - tient. The peo - ple — all shall

clear-ly — see how bad - ly you have treat - ed me. I'll — sue — for — sep - a -

The peo - ple all can clear - ly see

The peo - ple all can clear - ly see

The peo - ple all can clear - ly see

Oh, please be still, I want to flee.

peo - ple all can clear - ly see, can clear - ly see, how you have caused her

peo - ple all can clear - ly see, can clear - ly see, how you have caused her

peo - ple all can clear - ly see how you have caused her

peo - ple all can clear - ly see how you have caused her

peo - ple all can clear - ly see how you have caused her

sf sf sf sf sf

sue for_sep-a - ra - tion. You monster, you, too long have I been pa - - - -

win a sep-a - ra-tion. We nev-er heard such in-fa-my, too long has she been

win a sep-a - ra-tion. We nev-er heard such in-fa-my, too long has she been

joys of mar-ried sta - tion.

you have caused her mis-er-y. We nev-er heard such in-fa-my, too long has she been

you have caused her mis-er-y. We nev-er heard such in-fa-my, too long has she been

you have_caused her_ mis-er-y. You

you have caused her mis-er-y. You

you have caused her mis-er-y. You

- - tient. It is unheard. I'll sue for sep-a-ra - - - - - - tion.

pa - tient. The peo-ple all can clear-ly see she'll win a sep-a - ra-tion. We

pa - tient. The peo-ple all can clear-ly see she'll win a sep-a - ra-tion. We

Be still!   Enough!

pa - tient. The peo-ple all can clear-ly see she'll win a sep-a - ra-tion. We

pa - tient. The peo-ple all can clear-ly see she'll win a sep-a - ra-tion. We

brute.   You brute.

brute.   You brute.

brute.   You brute.

The peo-ple all can clear-ly see ——————— how bad-ly

nev - er heard such in - fa - my, too long has she been pa - tient. The peo - ple all can

nev - er heard such in - fa - my, too long has she been pa - tient. The peo - ple all can

Be still!

nev - er heard such in - fa - my, too long has she been pa - tient. The peo - ple all can

nev - er heard such in - fa - my, too long has she been pa - tient. The peo - ple all can

You brute.

You brute.

You brute.

You brute,

you have caused her mis - er - y. The

you have caused her mis - er - y. She'll win a sep - a - ra - tion. The

now the peo - ple all can see the joys of married sta - tion, of

She'll win a sep - a - ra - tion. The

you have caused her mis - er - y. She'll win a sep - a - ra - tion. The

pa - tient, you brute. _____ The

pa - tient, you brute. _____ The

pa - tient, you brute. _____ The

102

44163

ACT II

A room in the Garter Inn. A door at the center; two side doors, one of which leads to Falstaff's room. Tables with chairs and benches. Falstaff is discovered drinking with his neighbors.

Scene 1
No. 5 Song with Chorus

FALSTAFF: When still a child at my mother's breast, with hey-ho the wind and the rain, I drank my wine with skill and zest, for the rain there was rain-ing ev-e-ry day. Come hith-er, Jean-et Brown, come set the pitch-er down. Fill it a-new. Thirst can be like a flame, drinking is not a shame. Bacchus drank, too, yes, Bacchus drank, too. *(Falstaff says)* In position!

1st Neighbor: I can't anymore. (*falls down on Falstaff*)
Falstaff: Well, he is done for. Get him outside.

(*They put the 1st Neighbor on a bench and carry him out.*)

They car-ry one who had his fill. The wine at last has made him still. God Bac-chus gave him sooth-ing sleep. Your rest, poor man, be long and deep. Your rest, poor man, be long and deep.

Falstaff: More wine. I have to forget this awful taste of water.

44163

Falstaff:	Here goes another one. Get out, you drunkards, you offend my sense of modesty and virtue (*All the men exit.*)
Boy:	Sir John, a man is here who wants to see you. He brings a bottle of Madeira wine.
Falstaff:	A bottle of Madeira! Show him in.

Scene 2

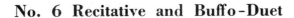

(Mr. Ford, pretending he is Mr. Brook, enters. Falstaff and Ford bow ceremoniously.

No. 6 Recitative and Buffo-Duet

Andante maestoso con moto

Recitative

MR. FORD

Good morning, sir. I am quite o-ver-

whelmed to meet here the ex-cellent and fa-mous John Fal-staff face to face. *(They bow again.)*

FALSTAFF *(flattered)* *(aside)* MR. FORD

You are too kind, sir. (What a charming man.) Most wor-thy sir, I was so bold to send this

FALSTAFF MR. FORD

bot-tle as a hum-ble present. Well, if you please, let's have a taste of it. I'm deep-ly

Andante

honored. To your health, dear sir.
(Falstaff pours the wine. *(They drink.)*
They toast each other.) To your health, dear sir. De - licious! Now, if I may know your

Andante

mf

MR. FORD   FALST. MR. FORD

name and what you want of me? My name is Brook, Brook? And I'm a man who earned and

Adagio

FALST.   MR. FORD

spent a lot. Then may I say to you: You've done as I did, too. But

p   *f*

still I've got a ti - dy sum of mon - ey, and I don't mind to spend it in an un - der-

FALSTAFF   MR. FORD

tak - ing for which I came to ask your kind as - sistance. A love adventure? Yes, that's

f

right. You, worthy sir, have earned a repu - ta - tion as a gal - lant man no la - dy can re-

p

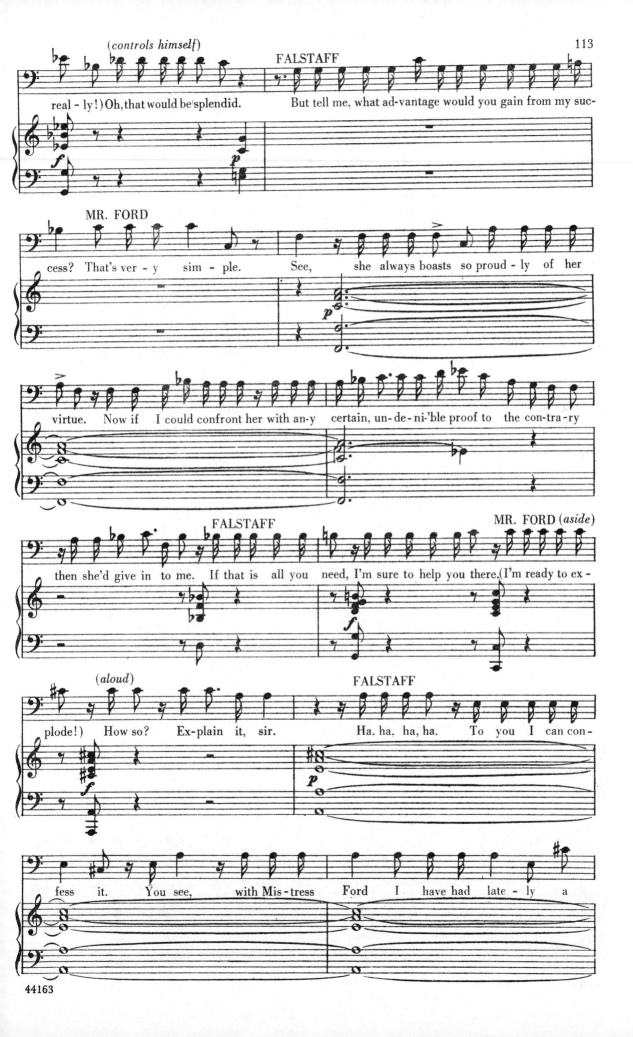

(controls himself)

FALSTAFF

real - ly!) Oh, that would be splendid. But tell me, what ad-vantage would you gain from my suc-

MR. FORD

cess? That's ver - y sim - ple. See, she always boasts so proud - ly of her

virtue. Now if I could confront her with an-y certain, un-de-ni-'ble proof to the con-tra-ry

FALSTAFF   **MR. FORD** (aside)

then she'd give in to me. If that is all you need, I'm sure to help you there. (I'm ready to ex -

(aloud)   **FALSTAFF**

plode!) How so? Ex-plain it, sir. Ha. ha. ha. ha. To you I can con-

fess it. You see, with Mis - tress Ford I have had late - ly a

44163

Buffo-Duet

Andante pesante

116

per - son - al - i - ty. I was covered up with laundry, dir - ty lin - en, hose and

sundry till the riv - er's i - cy flood cooled the ar - dour of my blood.

Yes, Sir Brook, i - mag - ine this big per - son - al - i -

MR. FORD

ty. Sir, my heart goes out to you.

Cruel it was what you went through. You have rea - son to com -

plain, sir, suff - 'ring in - ju - ry and pain there, for the love - ly Mistress

Poco meno mosso

Ford. There you see true love's reward, there you see true love's reward.

I - mag - ine.

Poco meno mosso

MR. FORD

Surely, after all you've met there, you are will-ing to for-

FALSTAFF

get her. Yes, almost. But let me say, if I want her she's mine to-

MR. FORD (*friendly*)

day. (Heavens, Hades! Quiet now!) What, so soon? Please tell me how.

FALSTAFF

Vic-to-ry, there's no de - bating, falls to men who please as I. And she's let me know she's

44163

FALSTAFF

MR. FORD

cur!) But I must be on my way. She'll be waiting till I get there. Everything will go much

FALSTAFF

MR. FORD

bet - ter. Eve - ry - thing will go much bet - ter. And we shall succeed to -

day.

I am hopeful and delight - ed.

And we shall suc - ceed to - day. I am hopeful and de -

Quick - ly, let us go a - way.

light - ed. Quick - ly, let us go a -

I am hopeful and de-light-ed, I am hope-ful and de-

way. I am hopeful and de - lighted, I am hope-ful and de-

lighted. Quickly let us go a - way, quickly let us go a-way, let's go a - way.

lighted. Quickly let us go a - way, quickly let us go a-way, let's go a - way. I

Allegretto moderato assai

FALSTAFF *sempre p*

sempre p

look a -head, I look a -head with keen an - tic - i - pa - tion. The woman will be

mine, I bet. We'll find our con - so - la - tion. Her husband, then, the sil - ly clown, shall

time has come when we must go a - way. _____ Now I am sure we shall succeed this ver-y

cresc.   *sf*   *f.*   *p.*

day. Yes, I am sure. Yes, I am sure we shall suc - ceed this ver - y

day. But now the time has come when we must go a - way. _____

sf   *p*   *cresc.*   *Ped.*

(embrace each other)   *a piacere*   (aside, still embracing him)

Fare - well sir. (I'll beat you black and brown.)   *lento*
p

Fare - well sir.   (He's

fp   *col canto*   *p*

124

Change of Scene

The garden of Mr. Page's house. Groups of trees and bushes. The house is seen in the background.

Scene 3

No. 7A Scene

Andantino quasi Allegretto

Curtain

SLENDER (*enters timidly*)

This is the hour when she is known to prom-e-nade each day.— Per-haps I'll see her quite a-lone when she will come this way.—O Anne, my dar-ling. I'll conceal my love no long-er. I'll speak to her with skill and

art. Have cour-age, Slen-der, now be brave. Don't
tremble so my heart. I know she'll see my pain so — grave. She can't re-main so
hard, she can't re-main so hard. There's someone coming.

Poco più mosso

It must be she. Now, courage. Oh heavens, no.

(hides behind a bush)

I can't. Oh dear, oh dear. I'll hide behind this bush, right here.

(*Cajus enters.*)

Tempo I DR. CAJUS

Je crois que now it is *cette-heur* Miss Anne to take her walk.— *Peut-*
et-re I can meet with her and have a lit-tle talk.— Ah, I shall
tell her *de ma propre bouche.* SLENDER Did he say "bush"? I fear he found me out. DR. CAJUS Yes, I shall

in tempo

spo-ken: Sweet Anne Page, *Je t'aime ter-ri-blement.* Where are my ri-vals?

In my rage I pierce them *ce moment.* Where are they now? Yes, in my rage, I pierce them

all. I pierce them *ce mo - ment.* Where are my ri - vals? I shall pierce them *ce mo -*

ment. I swear it *par honneur.* *Par ex - emple,* *ce miser-ab-le*

(*draws his sword*)

Slender. Where is he now, where is he now, where is he now? My sword here will make him even more

slen - der. And then *ce Mon-sieur* Fen - ton. I'll murder him, I'll murder him.

Andante

FENTON (*off-stage*)

Larks are singing high a - bove.

DR. CAJUS

Ciel qu'entends-je? It is Mon-sieur Fen-ton's voice.

Allegretto

(sheathes his sword and hides opposite the place where Slender is hiding)

I shall hide here *sans* a noise.

Scene 5

No. 7B Romance

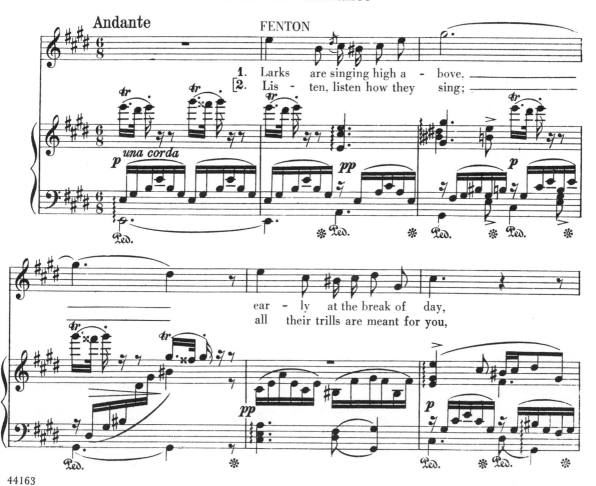

Andante

FENTON

1. Larks are singing high a - bove.
2. Lis - ten, listen how they sing;

una corda

ear - ly at the break of day,
all their trills are meant for you,

Scene 6

(Anne comes from the house. Slender and Cajus remain hidden.)

No. 7C Duet

be. Though my mother — of - ten — chided,

fa- ther scolded— me — be - fore, Long a - go— my— heart de-

cid- ed, Anne ——— will — be — your — own for - ev - er-

more. Dear - est heart, oh please for - give me, all my faith you did — re-

store. I'm so glad, ——— oh please, be-

No. 7D Quartet

(Anne goes off with Fenton. Cajus and Slender are dumbfounded. They run off.)

Curtain

Scene 7

(Change of Scene. Mistress Ford's room)

Falstaff: Mistress Ford, your sorrow has appeased my great suffering, and as a reward for your persistency I shall give you love so strong and delicious as only the gallant and heroic Sir John Falstaff can bestow. *(As he tries to embrace her a knock is heard at the door)*

Mrs. Page: Mistress Ford.

Falstaff: For heaven's sake, not again! Let me hide.

Mrs. Page: Are you alone?

Mrs. Ford: Why, what is the matter?

Mrs. Page: Your husband is in a tantrum. He has found out everything and he screams that he knows you have the knight here again. I am glad he is mistaken.

Mrs. Ford: Where is he now?

Mrs. Page: Just a few streets away and coming here fast.

Mrs. Ford: For heaven's sake, help us.

Mrs. Page: Then he is here again?

Mrs. Ford: Yes, he is.

Mrs. Page: Well, you certainly are in trouble. Let's put him in the basket.

Falstaff: *(entering)* No, I shall not go in the basket again. Help me to get out of here quickly.

Mrs. Ford: There is only one way. In there are clothes of my maid's aunt, the stout woman from Brainford. They will just fit you.

Falstaff: Oh, yes, anything rather than a fatality. *(He leaves)*

Mrs. Ford: This will work. My husband hates that woman and has sworn to beat her out of the house with a cudgel if she should ever set foot here again. Go in and disguise him well. *(Mrs. Page leaves)*
I hope everything goes well, this time.

Scene 8

No. 8 Duet

MR. FORD
sempre p

So, he's trapped and I shall

(Ford approaches slowly.)

catch him

Soon I'll grab him by the

nape.

From my hands she once could snatch him.

MRS. FORD

MR. FORD

cresc. What goes on?

(smugly)

This time,   this time,   this time,   this time,

Poco più mosso

So you feel a-gain vi-

though, he won't es-cape. No, this time he will not es-cape.

44163

Allegro

(*The two servants enter with the wash basket.*) MRS. FORD

Ah good!

I couldn't have planned it bet-ter. *f a piacere*

MR. FORD (*to the servants*)

Hey, you ras-cals, here you stay.

Moderato

col canto

Moderato

MR. FORD (*to her*) *f* (*to the servants*) (*They put the*

I'll in-spect ____ this pretty basket. Put it down where I can reach it. *basket down.*)

Ped. ✱

(*The servants want to leave,* *p*

Good. *but find the door locked.*) You look pale, what is the mat-ter?

fp *sf* *fp* *pp* Ped. ✱

MRS. FORD (*brazen*) **Allegro**

I? Of course, dear.

MR. FORD

Sending out your wash to bleach it? What a fancy

Allegro

fp *pp* Ped. ✱

lot. What a dirt-y lot. Wait,

wait. I'll wash ——— it on the spot. Say, what are you staring at? Id-iots! Oh

(notices the servants)

Moderato
(remembers)

(He lets the servants out and locks the door again.)

(heroically)

yes, I see. I locked the door behind me. So, now off with you. Now,

now I shall get your gallant lov-er so he can get a thorough washing. I'll

Allegro *(Starts furiously to take the laundry from the*

bleach, bleach_him of all col - or.

basket, and throws it around.)

Come out, come

No. 9 Finale

Allegro moderato

SLENDER *(outside)*
We're here, friend Ford, whom you have asked to come.

MR. FORD
Who's that?

DR. CAJUS *(outside)*
We're here, friend Ford, whom you have asked to come.

(knocking at the door)
MR. PAGE *(outside)*
We're here, friend Ford, whom you have asked to come.

Allegro moderato

MR. FORD
Ah yes. One mo-ment. *(opens the door)*

Scene 9

(They enter)
You all come in. O neighbors, how I'm put up-on by this un-

(Mrs. Ford calmly sits down.)
MR. PAGE
wor-thy shameless wom-an. Don't tell us you have found him, neighbor?

MR. FORD
Not

yet. She does not let me search the house. But all the same, right now ___ we'll go and

DR. CAJUS (*looking around*)

hunt him. *O ciel, quelle chose e-pou-van-ta-ble.* I must con-fess this is a ver-y pret-ty

MR. FORD

mess here. Just yes-ter-day you laughed at me. To-day you shall be

wit-ness-es of the re-venge ___ that I am taking.

MRS. FORD

I see you real-ly

mean it. Then I shall not resist your madness. Go search the house. I am re-signed to

44163

Scene 10

(Falstaff, disguised as an old woman, is led in by Mrs. Page.)

(Falstaff has been chased out.)

doubt. Ha ha ha ha ha ha ha ha! You'll en-joy it, I've no doubt.

doubt. Ha ha ha ha ha ha ha ha! You'll en-joy it, I've no doubt.

doubt. Out! Nev-er show your face a-gain, get out.

out, out. Nev-er show your face a-gain, get out.

out, out, out. Get out of here, get out, get out.

out, out, out. Get out of here, get out, get out.

Scene 11

Recitative

MR. FORD

So! She won't come a-gain, of that I'm cer-tain. Now look behind each trunk and cur-tain. If we today won't catch our fish then you may call me what you wish. Look out

full of ire that he could set the house on fire.

full of ire that he could set the house on fire.

full of ire that he could set the house on fire.

fast. I am full of ire I'll set the house on fire.

jeal - ous ire, I'll sure - ly set the house on fire.

(The men

hurry off in all directions.) Curtain

ACT III

A room in Mr. Page's house. There are two doors in the center and two tables. One table contains writing utensils. Around the other table Mr. and Mrs. Ford, Mr. and Mrs. Page, and Anne are seated. Mrs. Page is singing the Ballad.

Scene 1

No. 10 Ballad *

1. Of Herne, the hunt - er, I know a tale.   He
2. Of Herne, the hunt - er, I know a tale.   He's

*This Ballad may be omitted. If so, Act III begins with the Dialogue Scene, page 178

176

44163

*(Laugher is heard on the stage when the curtain rises, or applause,
if the ballad has been sung.)*

Page: What a wonderful trick you women played on the old sot.

Ford: Forgive me, dearest wife. I swear I shall never again doubt you.

Mrs. Page: But let us go through with our plan and punish him before the whole town.

Mrs. Ford: Yes, we shall send him a pair of horns and ask him to come to the haunted oak disguised as the hunter Herne.

Page: And we, with our neighbors, shall hide there and disguised as elves and goblins shall frighten him out of his wits.

Ford: And pinch him and beat him till he repents of his sins.

Mrs. Ford: Fine. Let us go and prepare everything.

Scene 2

Mrs. Page: *(to Anne as all the others exit)*
Listen, Anne, this masquerade is a perfect opportunity. I shall let Dr. Cajus know that you will wear this red elves costume. He will recognize you and you can elope and soon return as his wife. Good luck, my dear Mistress Doctor Cajus. *(Exit)*

Scene 3

Anne: Oh, heavens, what shall I do?

Page: *(enters furtively)* Are you alone? Here is your costume for tonight. Mister Slender will know that you are wearing the green elves mask. Run off with him. I have a priest waiting at the inn. You will surprise your mother when you return as Mistress Slender. Good luck, my dear daughter. *(Exit)*

Scene 4

Anne: Now I know what to do. I shall send the green costume to Dr. Cajus and the red one to Mr. Slender, and they will run off with each other. But I shall dress as Titania and ask Fenton to be my Oberon. Thus the plans of my parents shall help us to happiness.

No. 11 Aria

dolce
I so come near, my love, to you. When you ap-
proach you'll know me, too. Then we shall pledge our bond di-
cresc.
vine and you'll be mine, all mine.
mfp
p
p
There where the
tree - - tops soft - ly wave, we shall find shel-ter still and
Ped.

Change of Scene

Windsor Forest at night. In the background Herne's oak tree. Moonrise.

Scene 5

No. 12 Introduction and Chorus
(Moonrise)

Curtain

CHORUS

(Falstaff enters, disguised as Herne, with large antlers on his head.)

No. 13 Trio

FALSTAFF

The clock just struck the mid - night hour. This is the time she set. O Ju - pi - ter, for love you, too, wore horns up-on your head. If playing a bull was right for you then

44163

I'm ex-cused for what I do, then I'm ex-cused for _ what I do.

But now!

A rus-tle I can hear. I'm sure my lit - tle doe is near, I'm

sure my lit - tle doe is near.

Scene 7

(Mrs. Ford and Mrs. Page enter, hand in hand.)

MRS. FORD

Pst, pst! Pst, pst! Sir John!

193

44163

(leading Mrs. Page to him)

It's Meg, — my heart, she came with me. MRS. PAGE

I could no

tree.

more resist your charms. I had to fly in-to your arms. FALSTAFF

in tempo

col canto

Now, come raging

cresc.

storms, furious weath-er; sul - phur pour down by night and by day.

Poco meno mosso

Here we'll build our nest togeth-er and I'll nev-er go a-way, Here we'll build our nest togeth-er

(to one) (to the other)

Tempo I

and — I'll nev - er, nev-er go a-way.

ritard.

Scene 9

(Elves and Spirits)

Ballet and Chorus of Elves

gay. You elves in white and red and gray, your dance be merry, fast and gay.

Scene 10

(*Anne, dressed as Titania, is brought in on a carriage.*)

Andante

ANNE
dolce assai

The world's — a - sleep, — we're safe from hu - man

eyes._ So let_ us walk_ where fragrant flow - ers rise._ We

shall_ en - joy_ the nightin-gale's sweet tone;_ O come_ to me,_ be -

lov - ed O - be - ron._

CHORUS

Soprano *pp*

The world's_ a - sleep._

Alto *pp*

Scene 11

(Fenton, dressed as Oberon, enters from the other side.)

Andante

Andante

mfp

206

gain I'm your Ti - ta - ni - a, And now a-gain I'm your Ti - ni -

gain you're mine. Ti - ni - a, And now again you're mine, Ti - ta - ni -

saw. And now a - gain, a - gain she's your Ti - ni -

(They go off, hand in hand.)

a.

a.

a.

a. — The hour has come.

Allegro come primo

And now, again, let's make the rounds   through

Allegro come primo

Windsor forest's air-y grounds,
Through woods and brush, by

Scene 12

(Page, disguised as Herne, enters with others masked as spirits.)

bloom and thorn. Come hunter Herne and blow your horn, blow your horn, blow your horn. Blow your horn,

Blow. *(Herne tries in vain to blow his horn.)* in tempo *(Herne tries again

blow your horn. Come, blow your horn.

but the horn does not sound.)* in tempo MR. PAGE Andante a piacere

No sound comes to my ear. I feel a man is

Don't wait, so blow your horn.

Recitative *lento*
MR. PAGE

Scene 13

Dance of the Insects

No. 16 General Dance and Chorus

Recitative

MR. PAGE

As he still will not repent, torture him, the mis-creant. Come you spirits, small and big. Go at him and stab and

Scene 14

(Many people in masks, others dressed as spirits, storm in and torture Falstaff in diverse ways.)

Allegro

CHORUS

Tenor

Fie on sin-ful fan-ta-sy, and fie on lust and lux-u-ry.

Bass

Fie on sin-ful fan-ta-sy, and fie on lust and lux-u-ry.

Lust is but a blood-y fire, is kindled by un-chaste de-sire.

Lust is but a blood-y fire, is kindled by un-chaste de-sire.

Letter writing, husband spiting, will provoke our in-ter-cession. You'll be strangled, bad-ly mangled

Letter writing, husband spiting, will provoke our in-ter-cession. You'll be strangled, bad-ly mangled

if you don't re-pent. Vicious traitor, vi-o-la-tor. bad-ly mangled.

You'll be strangled,

if you don't re-pent. vi-o-la-tor. bad-ly mangled.

if you don't re-pent. Vicious traitor, You'll be strangled,

Tenor
Fie on sin-ful fan-ta-sy, and fie on lust and lux-u-ry. Lust is
Bass
Lust is

but a blood-y fire, is kin-dled by un-chaste desire.

but a blood-y fire, is kin-dled by un-chaste desire.

He who tries to de - ceive oth-er peo - ple oft him-self is _ caught in his net.

He who tries to de - ceive oth-er peo - ple oft him-self is _ caught in his net.

If it's wom-en you would in - vei - gle you'll need a smart - er brain in your

If it's wom-en you would in - vei - gle you'll need a smart - er brain in your

head. Pinch him, burn him, stab him.

head. Pinch him, burn him, stab him. Hy - - - a,

Hy - - - - - a. Vicious traitor, vi - o - la - tor.

hy - - - - a. Vi - o - la - tor.

Vicious traitor, vicious traitor.

Scene 15

(Falstaff jumps up, throws away his antlers and tries to run off. All the principals, except Cajus and Slender, bar his way.)

Falstaff: Pity, pity, I repent.

Mrs. Page: Then you shall meet my husband, Mister Page.

Mrs. Ford: And this is—

Falstaff: Mister Brook, my friend.

Ford: Oh no, I am Mister Ford and not your friend.

Mrs. Ford: Sir John, we did not have any luck. I will never be your love but think you are a dear.

Falstaff: I begin to perceive that I am nothing but an ass.

Mr. Slender: Mister Page, Mister Page, see here, I married Dr. Cajus.

Dr. Cajus: *Mort de ma vie* who made such a fool of me?

Mrs. Page: I have a suspicion. Where is Anne and Mister Fenton?

Fenton: Here we are, husband and wife.

Anne: Pardon, good father; dearest mother, pardon.

Mrs. Page: I see true love prevailed against our plans. Dear children, here is my blessing.

Page: And mine, too. Let us all be happy.

230

44163

End of the opera